Make More
of Squashes
• • •

Patricia Harbottle

•

Peter Chadwick

•

Elisabeth Winkler

Make More of Squashes
© Patricia Harbottle, Peter Chadwick and Elisabeth Winkler

ISBN: 978-1-906316-37-2.

Published in 2009 by HotHive Books, Evesham, UK.
www.thehothive.com

A CIP record of this book is available from The British Library.

Printed in the UK by TJ International, Padstow.

h⸬thivebooks

About the authors

• • •

Patricia Harbottle's lifelong love of the culinary arts climaxed with the establishment of her thriving catering enterprise in London; latterly she created a highly successful wine-related business. On moving to Dorset she pursued her interest in food, from its provenance, production and preparation to its presentation.

Peter Chadwick has been a horticultural explorer for over 40 years and his professional life is involved with the field scale production of vegetables. He lives in Worcestershire and plays the saxophone when he is not growing crops.

Elisabeth Winkler is passionate about eating for health. What could be more brimming with goodness than fresh produce you have grown yourself? Editor of the Soil Association magazine, *Living Earth*, for seven years, she is now food editor for the green magazine, *The Source*. Elisabeth's food blog (realfoodlover.wordpress.com) was shortlisted for the 2009 Guild of Food Writers Awards.

Patricia's thank yous

. . .

Sarah
I got to know Sarah Langton-Lockton because we share a love of jigsaw puzzles. My former catering partner Michelle, who has also contributed to this and other books in the series, created a small jigsaw puzzle club a few years ago and we meet for a fun evening every now and again. Sarah has an allotment where she grows all manner of vegetables organically.

Sinnet
Sinnet Morch is a good, long-standing friend who lives in London. She was a tremendous help to me in my wine-related antiques business days. She is a Dane with a great knowledge of the food of her native country.

Jo
Some people may remember Jo Andrews as the senior political correspondent on "News at Ten". She has travelled extensively throughout the world. She is a very much treasured member of our large family and is a keen, inspirational cook.

Jen
My wonderfully inspirational American friend, Jennifer Bushman, culinary author, cookery school creator and TV personality is a tower of strength and support in my creative efforts. Her intriguing recipes throughout this series will become favourite dishes of many.

Michelle

I have known Michelle Berriedale-Johnson for over 30 years. She and I set up a catering company in London – Catercall – in the 1970s, building it up into a thriving operation until we sold it to take up other interests. She is the author of numerous cookery books, including two for the British Museum, and the Editor of the only English magazine for allergy problems – *Foods Matter*. Check out her website www.foodsmatter.com.

Anna

Anna del Conte is a household name to anyone remotely interested in cooking. She is the queen of Italian cookery writers. I got to know her while living in London, and much better once we moved to live near each other in the country. It was she who had the idea for this series and graciously allowed us to take on the task of producing the books for it. She has just published her memoirs, *Risotto with Nettles* (Chatto and Windus), documenting her full and fascinating life, including some of her favourite recipes.

Foreword

by Anna Del Conte

• • •

Whenever I had a meal at the Harbottles I always noticed that the vegetables were never treated just as an accompaniment to the meat or the fish; they were never served just like that, plain, steamed or boiled; they were always properly cooked and even more properly finished off, a treat in their own right.

So when Pat Harbottle told me that she was going to write a series of books on vegetables, I knew that all the recipes would be winners. I would no longer have to ask Pat "and do you mind telling me how you cooked those delicious courgettes?" But what I didn't know was how comprehensive this little book is. It is dedicated to pumpkins and squash in all their varieties and shapes: how to plant and grow them from seed, how to feed and nurture them, how to store them and finally how to cook them.

The cultivating section of the book has been written by Peter Chadwick, a horticulturist, and Elisabeth Winkler. Peter spells out very clearly anything and everything you need or want to know about the technical side of growing the vegetables, plus how, where and when to buy and what to look for when you do that.

The 50 recipes which follow are a joy to read and I am sure an even bigger joy to eat. Some are of utter simplicity, such as the most perfect prosciutto and melon (served here as a cocktail bite), while some are more complicated like a sophisticated recipe for little timbales of courgette served with a clean and sharp tomato salsa.

This book will be followed by a book on roots, a book on lettuce and chicory, brassica, and so on. All the vegetables will be included in this attractive series and, if the first book, *Make More of Beans & Peas*, is anything to go by, I feel that when I have the whole series I will become a complete vegetarian.

Anna Del Conte, May 2009, Dorset

Contents

. . .

Make More of Vegetables

by Elisabeth Winkler and Peter Chadwick

Growing
Pumpkins & Squashes

• • •

The stars of this show are pumpkins and squashes. Pumpkins are a member of the squash family, which also includes butternut squash, melon, watermelon, cucumber, courgettes and marrows. Mostly annual plants with showy blossoms, squashes are the edible members of the Cucurbitaceae family.

Pumpkins are a familiar sight at Halloween used as carved orange lanterns. But their role as a super-food is less renowned. Pumpkins, like all squashes, have highly nutritional health-giving properties. That, coupled with their adaptability to most types of cuisine, deserves to put pumpkins and squashes firmly in the limelight.

Cultivated in Central America thousands of years ago, squashes were one of the Three Sisters planted by Native Americans – the other two were maize and beans. An essential food resource wherever they are grown, squashes contain vital amounts of gentle soluble fibre, immune-boosting vitamins and minerals, as well as complex carbohydrates, providing sustainable, slow release (yet low-fat) energy.

Growing pumpkin and squashes is perfect for beginner gardeners. Their seeds are large, robust and easy-to-handle, and they germinate readily in the warmth of a south-facing windowsill.

Winter and summer squashes

Squashes are divided into two types, winter and summer. Summer squashes are harvested young before their skins get tough, while winter ones take longer to mature.

Winter squashes
The winter types, such as pumpkin, butternut or acorn squashes, can be eaten during winter when little else is available. They are left to mature on the plant until it dies in autumn or a frost is likely, whichever happens first. Most winter squashes can be stored for up to six months indoors in a dry, cool (10–15°C) atmosphere. Winter squashes have harder skins

and denser flesh so are harder to peel, take longer to cook and are also sweeter than summer ones. Thinly cut winter squashes can be steamed, boiled or fried, or roasted whole (or halved) in the oven for 40 minutes – they are easier to peel and chop when tender and done.

Winter squash is one of the few vegetables to keep its nutritional quality after picking. Equalling carrots for health, they are a top source of vitamin A with good amounts of vitamin C, folate and soluble fibre, as well as potassium and manganese. Orange-fleshed types such as pumpkin are rich in beta-carotene – the deeper the colour, the more carotene you are getting.

Summer squashes
Summer squashes such as courgettes or cucumbers, are best eaten fresh off the vine. They are succulent, with soft skins and a mild flavour. Very fresh squashes may not need peeling and are easy to cut-up small. Some types, such as cucumber, don't even need cooking, while the rest can get away with the lightest touch, such as steaming or stir-frying.

Summer squash is a top source of the mineral manganese and vitamin C. It is low in calories yet packs a nutritional punch with good amounts of vitamin A, folate and soluble fibre, as well as potassium, magnesium and phosphorus.

Growing courgettes for beginners

This mini-guide shows you how to grow courgettes in outdoor containers. Courgettes are a summer squash. Varieties commonly grown in the UK are compact and bushy (not trailing) so are most suited for container growing.

Courgettes, like all squashes, have large seeds that are robust and easy to handle – perfect for beginners. In turn they produce vigorous seedlings and plants. We show you how to start the seeds indoors to ensure a summer crop, as early as June. Well-adapted to the British climate, courgettes can be grown in containers on a sunny spot – no need for a garden. We suggest you aim for four plants to feed four people through the summer months, weather permitting. You will need four containers, one for each plant.

Courgettes must be picked before they get too big so it won't be long before you enjoy your first courgette meal. Regular picking is especially important when growing in containers – they won't cope well with big, heavy fruit to support. Site the containers near the kitchen if possible to keep an eye on them, and for ease of watering and picking.

Timing and biology

You sow the seeds indoors in late spring, and by summer your grown-up plants live outdoors, first producing yellow flowers then courgettes. The more you pick, the more courgettes your plant will produce. It's biology: the plant's aim is to reproduce – produce seeds – before it dies. Cutting a courgette interrupts the reproduction cycle and tricks the plant into thinking it has not managed to produce any seed. So the plant redoubles its breeding efforts, making more flowers to become courgettes.

Courgette plants can produce fruit from late June until the first frost of autumn, or powdery mildew kills them (more prevalent when it's rainy). The cropping season generally finishes around the autumn equinox, mid-September.

The birds and bees

Growing courgettes is a lesson in reproduction. Every courgette plant carries both male and female flowers. Courgettes are 'born' thanks to bees taking pollen from male flowers to female ones – after successful pollination, the embryo on the female flower develops into a courgette. In nature the bee's success is accidental. The gardener can take control of the process by introducing pollen by hand from male to female flowers. Children will love to help you because this is a natural explanation of conception. (see 'Helping pollination' on p18).

Cost-cutting

Don't invest huge sums of money in growing. Your care and attention is what counts.

Collect eight used yogurt pots, or similar, all about the same size: 10cm/4 inch in diameter for growing the seedlings indoors. Your pots need to be sturdy enough to withstand watering, and big-enough for a good amount of compost to house the growing seed. Yogurt pots are perfect but you need to punch several holes in the bottom for drainage. Heat a sharp knife tip (or a nail held by pliers) over a gas flame and make holes with its red-hot tip.

Courgette plants have large leaves on brittle stems and are heavy when the courgettes start to grow. This makes the plants top-heavy so don't skimp on container-size as it can act as ballast if the wind gets blowy once the plants are transferred outdoors. Your container needs to be able to hold 10 litres of compost – one of the very big bags.

The most economical big containers are builders' buckets, which can be bought from most hardware stores. The other advantage is they are light to carry home. If you can, remove the bucket's handles. You must have drainage holes in the bottom of the bucket (six holes about 1cm diameter each) and can make them with a drill.

Another cheap alternative is an empty coffee bean sack (from a coffee bar).

For cheap compost, buy growbags from a garden centre or hardware shop. If you choose the organic version you will be helping to preserve peat bogs. Split the bags open, mix the contents with some garden soil that has had the lumps crushed and the large stones picked out, and empty the mixture into your buckets or containers. The added soil will improve the retention of water and nutrients, and help stabilise the container when it is windy.

Sowing seeds

Generally sow your seeds towards the end of April. There is no benefit in sowing earlier as you will end up with leggy seedlings if kept too long indoors. Generally, start sowing at the end of April if you live in the south, while northerners wait till early May. You are aiming to get your seedlings living permanently outdoors on their tray in time for the warm days of mid or late-May.

List for sowing seeds

Get ready at the start of April for sowing your seeds indoors by collecting everything you need:

Collect eight 10cm pots (see 'Cost-cutting' on p13) or similar containers with good drainage.

A packet of courgette seeds from a garden centre, hardware store or online supplier. (See 'Support' on p21 for information on hybrid or traditional varieties and 'Suitable varieties for container growing' on p22).

A seed tray to hold them or something similar with drainage holes. Drainage holes are vital because you don't want your pots standing in a puddle that will cause the compost to become waterlogged. Seed trays are cheap, the right size and reusable for years.

50 litres of organic potting compost from a growbag. You will use a little for sowing the seeds in pots, and the rest for the big containers.

Sowing 'recipe'

We are aiming for four plants but starting with 16 seeds. Not all will survive – it's a tough world.

1. Pre-soak your 16 courgette seeds to speed up germination (when the seed comes to life). Cover them in cold water and soak the seeds for eight hours – no more.

2. Place the 16 soaked seeds between several layers of damp kitchen towel in a large-enough dish.

3. Put the dish in a plastic bag, fold the open end under the dish and keep at a steady 20°C – your kitchen is warm enough, or a heated airing cupboard.

4. Check your seeds daily and as soon as a root is visible (after a few days) the seed needs to be sown in its pot so the fledgling plant can quickly gain nourishment from the compost. Have your eight pots ready on a tray with drainage holes.

5. Fill each pot with compost. Then gently press the soaked seed into the compost, root down, two seeds per pot. The seeds need to be about 3cm beneath the compost, but no deeper, so the seed does not have to grow too far to reach the light. Now crumble in some more compost, enough to cover the seed (like pulling the curtains at night), gently pressing the compost to bed down the seed. Be careful when pushing the seed into the compost, you don't want to damage the emerging root.

6. Keep the tray as near as possible to natural light, ideally on a south-facing windowsill. For now your seeds are staying indoors.

7. Once the seedlings have emerged and their first smooth oval leaves are opened flat, pull out the weaker of the two in each pot (assuming they have both germinated). Generally the first seedlings to appear make stronger plants, so if in doubt choose the one which emerged first. Like all squashes, courgettes produce a biggish root, so it is best to remove the weaker seedling before it gets too big and might interfere with the growth of the stronger one.

Looking after your seeds indoors

The roots of the baby seedlings descend seeking water and food while the stems grow up towards the light. After about two weeks you should see the first stem emerging. Your main concern is keeping the compost in the pots moist but not waterlogged. There is no need to add more nutrients.

Your parenting skills are developing awareness of temperature and light on behalf of your young charges. Your aim is to have your emerging seedlings outside as soon as possible for bursts of the real world of wind, rain and sun.

Once the second pair of leaves has opened fully, it's time to move the young plants in their pots from indoors to outdoors. Start getting them used to being outdoors about mid-May (or end of May for the north of the UK). Move the tray outside to a sheltered place for a few hours of sun but always bring it in at night. It's rather like giving a baby in a pram some fresh air every day.

Keep an eye open for which plants develop their leaves first – as we saw earlier with the seedlings, generally the first to develop make for the strongest plants. You may have eight young plants growing indoors but only four will be planted outdoors in containers. Start deciding which ones will make the strongest plant.

The last frost of spring

Eventually you want that tray outdoors all night. But when will it be warm enough for your baby seedlings? Low night temperatures slow-down the plant's metabolism so don't put them outside too early. You need to wait until the risk of a frosty night has passed – the end of May for the south, or mid-June for the north.

A plant needs an equable temperature to thrive; that means warm nights as well as days to make your plants feel comfortable enough to flower – an average of 16 degrees over a period of 24 hours for courgettes. It generally does not get too hot in the UK but it can get too cold and that's what you have to watch out for. Ask a neighbour for local advice about the last frost, if unsure.

Shopping list for planting outdoors

- 4 x builders' buckets or other suitable containers big enough for 10 litres of compost each. You need to make 1cm diameter drainage holes in the base of your containers if they don't already have them;

- One packet of blood, fish and bone, or a general purpose slow-release fertiliser suitable for vegetarians/vegans, to add to the container's compost three weeks after planting out your seedlings. (see 'Food' on p19);

- Extract of seaweed in liquid form. Once diluted with water, it is a weekly nutrient-boost to spray on the courgette's leaves (see 'Food' on p19);

- Two plastic sprayers, one for the nutrient-boost, the other to make a simple anti-pest spray using washing-up liquid (see 'Organic methods of dealing with pests' on p20); and

- Self-watering device (optional – see 'Water' on p19).

Time to plant outdoors

The tray and small pots are a temporary billet. Once the seedling has produced a pair of true leaves (actually the second pair, the first does not count), it is time to be planted in its next and final home. When the time comes to move the young courgette plant from its yogurt pot to a big container, the roots should be embedded in enough compost to avoid over-handling.

A squash plant is sensitive to root-damage so be ever so calm and gentle when transplanting it.

1. Fill the four containers with your compost/prepared garden soil mixture.

2. Scoop out a hole big enough to accommodate your transplant.

3. Choose your strongest four young plants (see 'Looking after your seeds indoors' on p16) and water each one in its small pot.

4. Handling it gently, turn the small pot upside down with the plant's stem between the base of your index and middle finger. Gently tap the bottom of the pot with the other hand to dislodge the root ball. Once the plant is free of the pot, carefully turn it upright and place it in its new home in the big container.

5. Press the compost around the transplant without damaging the roots too much.

6. Your young plant should be deep enough in its new home so that the lowest leaves are on the surface of the compost. Then firm the soil around the seedling to gently bed it in.

Helping pollination

Each courgette plant has male and female flowers. Courgettes are rarely short of insect visitors because their flowers are so big and bright. But it is fun to help pollination along by transferring the pollen by hand from male to female flowers on any of your courgette plants.

In nature, the transfer of pollen is usually made by bees. When one visits a male flower, pollen sticks to its furry body. If the bee then visits a female flower, this pollen is transferred to the female's sticky stigma. Then a baby-fruit can be conceived.

Male and female flowers are easy to identify because they are different. Male flowers grow on long stems and are often carried above the plant's leaves to attract insect pollinators. Female flowers have a swelling on the stem behind the petals. This is the embryo which will develop into the fruit after successful pollination.

Wait until the plant is carrying open flowers of both sexes simultaneously.

Cut a male flower from the plant, remove its petals and rub its pollen tip gently over the stigma of the female flower.

Plenty of pollen is produced by the male so its pollen is easy to see.

The stigma is sticky so the pollen will stay put.

You will also be able to tell if you successfully transferred the pollen to the female stigma because the embryo fruit behind the flower will begin to swell after a couple of days.

Caring for your growing plant – food, water and support

Once your young plants are bedded in their containers, temperature is no longer an issue. Your focus shifts to the compost. This gives the plant food and water and it's your job to make sure it has enough of both. Due to restricted space in containers, you have to water well and feed well.

Here's how:

Water

It's easy to have good watering intentions and as easy to forget them; then make up for neglect with a water binge. Watering – either over or under – is probably the biggest cause of failure with container-growing. As with the seed's first pots, the compost in the container has to be moist but not waterlogged.

Timing can be a problem. The main cropping period (when the fruits are ready to be picked) starts in August – which usually coincides with people being away on holiday. Luckily there are some cheap and ingenious contraptions available from hardware shops, garden centres and online. Self-watering devices usually consist of a plastic bag or small tank to hold water, some sort of dripper which goes into the container's soil and some flexible tubing to join the two. You can also get devices that are fixed to an empty bottle (then filled with water). The bag, tank or bottle is raised above the surface of the soil. The height difference can be adjusted to vary the application rate. This system is really useful if you are the sort of person who forgets to water plants.

You can also make your own watering-device with a plastic bottle. Search on the internet or visit **http://tinyurl.com/bbuvp6** for instructions.

Food

Your courgettes will need extra food because they are growing in containers. Normally courgette plants are shallow rooting, gathering nutrients from the soil. In containers, their roots can only spread out so far so they need some extra help from you.

Use a fertiliser approved for organic gardening because of its slow-release action. Three weeks after planting the young plants in their grown-up homes, add dry organic nutrients, such as blood, fish and bone, or any other slow-release general-purpose fertiliser suitable for vegetarians/vegans. Use about 50g in total or two tablespoons per container. Mix this into the top 3cm of soil in each container; an old dinner fork is the ideal tool. And do wash your hands and any kitchen utensils you use afterwards. Repeat four weeks later.

Once your plants are growing strongly, give them a weekly nutrient-boosting feed. This is especially important once the plants start to flower to maximise the chances of a fertilised flower bearing its fruit.

Every week spray the courgette leaves with liquid seaweed feed that has been diluted with water. Apart from providing basic plant nutrients, foliar feeds provide the plants with lots of other useful nutrients: for example they can help stimulate the plant's defence mechanism against pests and disease. The most effective foliar feeds, whether organically approved or not, come from organic (once-living) sources such as seaweed. Dilute with water, according to the instructions on the packet. Chase Organics specialises in extract of seaweed – see the mini-appendix at the end of this chapter.

Organic methods of dealing with pests

All squash plants are covered with hairs to some extent. These offer some protection from pests as the hairs on courgette plants are stiff and sharp.

The use of collars cut from large mineral water bottles and placed around the base of the plant will usually take care of slugs. Once the plant is well established, it does not suffer from these pests.

If aphids (greenfly) attack your courgettes, spray the plants with soapy water. Squirt a couple of drops of washing-up liquid in enough water to make it foamy, and fill a hand spray. The soapiness disrupts the aphid's waxy skin. Sometimes the force of the water is enough to dislodge the tiny pests.

What are pests to us is food for insects such as ladybirds. Soon natural systems will kick-in to protect your plants. Hungry for meat such as aphids and other garden-pests, the intrepid ladybird will fly far hunting for food, right up to a high-rise balcony.

Strictly speaking, the mighty aphid eaters are ladybird larvae. The adults find the aphid colonies and lay their eggs among the pest – food for the 'baby' ladybird. Aphids are also food for tiny wasps which lay an egg inside an aphid. When the egg hatches, the wasp larva eats the pest. You can recognise empty aphid bodies by their shiny, metallic appearance and the tiny hole in the abdomen drilled by the wasp to enable it to escape.

Wasps are good news in early summer when they are from a young colony and bug-hunting so leave them alone to do their thing. By late summer they are more interested in a sugary fruity diet, and then become a nuisance.

Take note

Keep notes of when and how your seedlings and crops perform. Don't forget to date the entries. Your notes will be useful for the following year.

Support

Unless you go out of your way to buy traditional or heirloom seeds, you probably bought seed of an F1 hybrid. F1 seeds are a type of seed produced under controlled conditions away from its natural parents. This method of seed production ensures the ensuing plants are reliable – they grow uniformly and vigorously (for the first crop only; F1 seeds have to be bought anew each year). So if the packet tells you it has a compact bushy habit, you can be sure that every plant will be like that.

If you choose a courgette variety which is an open-pollinated (non-F1 hybrid) variety, expect to see some differences in the growth habit of your plants. Some of the less cultivated plants may trail more and start to spill over the edge of your containers. Don't worry about this but make sure there is enough space around each container for the trailers to continue growing on the ground.

From now on, training, watering and feeding are the only tasks required until picking starts. The first flowers should appear at the end of June. They will produce their first fruits by about late-June. Feel free to pick them early to try them at different stages and see how they taste. You can't harm the plant – the opposite. As we have said, picking the fruits encourages the plant to produce more.

So pick and enjoy!

Suitable varieties for container growing

Traditional or open-pollinated varieties:

All Green Bush

Genovese

Bambino

F1 varieties:

Midnight F1
(claimed to be spineless)

Tuscany F1

Tempra F1

Venus F1

One Ball (yellow fruits)

Soleil F1 (yellow fruits)

Black Forest F1 – if you want to grow a trailing type on a trellis or fence. Trailing types will grow unsupported but will cover a lot of ground.

A few tips on preparing winter squashes

Many people miss out on using squashes, particularly winter ones, because some are not easy to prepare. I hope that these few tips will help you get over the problem and enjoy the great vegetable that they are.

It is best to tackle the job with a sharp thin-bladed but strong carving knife. The less width you have on the knife, the easier it will be to penetrate the tough outer case. Insert the point first, then press down in an arc and the knife will go through the skin easier. After the first cut life gets a lot simpler.

Another problem can be that some squashes are reluctant to give up their seeds together with their 'umbilical cord', the threadlike membrane. Again the thin knife comes in useful. Just run it under the start of the flesh and then scrape the centre out. It will come away easily.

Useful suppliers

Organic gardening catalogue
Tel. 0845 130 1304 http://www.organiccatalog.com/catalog/

Chase Organics
Tel. 01932 253666 http://www.chaseorganics.co.uk

Recipes

(to serve 4 unless otherwise stated)

by Patricia Harbottle

Soups
&
Starters

Jen's butternut squash soup

When I emailed my brilliant American friend, Jennifer Bushman, to tell her I was researching this book, I got an immediate message back – "I made a butternut squash soup for our Thanksgiving dinner tonight. It has hints of curry and is finished with crème fraîche and toasted hazelnuts. I will write it down and send it to you." A wonderfully generous offer. I hope you'll love it as much as I do.

1 large butternut squash
750g (1lb 10oz) skin-on pumpkin wedges or 1 small whole pumpkin
10g (½oz) unsalted butter
125g (4½oz) chopped onion
500ml (17fl oz) warmed vegetable or chicken stock
½ tablespoon curry powder
½ tablespoon runny honey
100ml (3½fl oz) double cream
Salt and freshly ground black pepper to taste
Crème fraîche thinned slightly with milk or olive oil
1 tablespoon chopped toasted hazelnuts

Cut the squash (and small pumpkin if using) in half and remove the membrane and seeds. Reserve the pumpkin seeds. Put the vegetables in a baking tin with a small amount of water in the bottom and bake in a 190°C (170°C for a fan oven) or Gas Mark 5 for about an hour until very soft.

Meanwhile melt the butter over a medium heat. Add the onion and sauté slowly until soft but not brown. Remove the flesh from the squash and pumpkin and place in a processor with the butter and onion. Purée until smooth, adding the warmed stock gradually. Pour the soup into a medium pan. Add the curry powder, honey and cream and season to taste. Heat through and serve in bowls, garnished with a dollop of crème fraîche and some chopped toasted hazelnuts.

The pumpkin seeds can easily be made into a tasty snack. (Recipes page 36 & 90.)

Marrow and ham soup

1.2 litres (2 pints) any unsalted stock or water
1 small cooked ham shank
120g (4oz) roughly chopped onion
175g (6oz) peeled roughly chopped old potato
225g (8oz) marrow in 1cm (½ inch) cubes
150ml (¼ pint) single cream
Freshly ground black pepper

If you have an old, tough skinned marrow you may have to peel it, but try to avoid that if you can as the skin looks so pretty in the soup. You could always stir in some chopped parsley instead.

Put the stock in a large pan with the ham shank, onion and potato. Bring to the boil and simmer for 30 minutes until the vegetables are tender. Remove the shank from the pan together with any meat from it. Pour the stock into a blender or food processor and blend until really smooth.

Remove the meat from the ham bone and shred 80g (3oz) of it very finely. Pour the liquid into a clean pan, add the marrow and simmer for 3 minutes. Add the ham and cream and heat through. Season to taste and serve sprinkled with chopped parsley.

Cucumber broth

There seem to be endless recipes for chilled cucumber soup so I put my mind to something light but hot…

450g (1lb) cucumber, peeled, cut lengthways and deseeded
25g (1oz) butter
1 large finely chopped onion
1 large clove finely chopped garlic
50g (2oz) chopped celery stalk
1.2 litres (2 pints) well-flavoured chicken stock
4–8 drops Tabasco
1–2 teaspoons Marigold vegetable bouillon or
some crumbled stock cube
A little salt and freshly ground black pepper

Take the long halved pieces of peeled cucumber and slice them down the middle again then slice the quarters crossways into 1cm (½ inch) thick crescents.

Melt the butter in a large pan and gently fry the onion and garlic for 5 minutes until soft. Add the cucumber and celery, put the lid on the pan and sweat the vegetables for another 5–10 minutes. Pour in the chicken stock and simmer the mixture for about 15 minutes until the vegetables are cooked, leaving the cucumber with a little crunch.

If you think your stock needs extra flavour, add some vegetable bouillon or stock cube. Season further with salt, pepper and Tabasco to taste.

Should you wish to garnish the soup, the best option is to float some flakes of toasted onion on top.

Seafood stuffed melon

2 Ogen or other small melons
120g (4oz) peeled cooked prawns
120g (4oz) hot-smoked trout fillet
120g (4oz) white crabmeat
6 tablespoons homemade or good quality bought mayonnaise
Juice of 1 lime
Freshly ground black pepper
Parsley to garnish

Cut the melons in half, stalk side down and remove the seeds. If the halves do not sit well, slice a small amount off the bottom to stabilise them. If your prawns have been frozen, make sure they are well drained of liquid.

Divide the trout into large flakes and put into a bowl with the prawns and crabmeat. Stir the lime juice into the mayonnaise together with the black pepper and mix with the fish to coat it well. Spoon the fish mixture into the melon cavities, piling it up attractively. Garnish with chopped parsley or just a sprig if preferred.

Cucumber, melon and leek flan

My great friend, Michelle, sent me a recipe that inspired me to create this unusual flan. Her recipe is delicious but not quite suitable for this book on squashes.

1 x 20cm (8 inch) shortcrust pastry case, baked blind until
fully cooked and light brown
2 tablespoons sunflower oil
175g (6oz) washed, trimmed and sliced leeks
1–2 medium hot, deseeded, finely sliced red chillies
250g (9oz) deseeded, diced cucumber
150g (5oz) wedge of skinned melon, cut across in slices
100g (3½oz) thinly sliced Gruyère or Emmenthal cheese
Freshly ground black pepper

Heat the oil in a wide, lidded pan and gently cook the leeks and chilli until they begin to soften, about 5 minutes. Add the cucumber and sweat with the lid on for about 10 minutes. Remove from the heat and tip the vegetables and melon into the pastry case. They should be domed up in the middle. Lay the cheese slices over the top, covering the whole pie. Bake at 180°C (160°C for a fan oven) or Gas Mark 4 for about 15 minutes until the cheese is melted and browned. Grind black pepper over the top when it comes out of the oven.

This is nicest served warm but you can enjoy it cold, too.

Melon, avocado and apricot salad

1 medium Galia melon
1 large avocado
Juice of 1 lemon
8 soft, no-soak, dried apricots
6 tablespoons olive oil
Pinch of sugar
A big handful of mint, chopped
A little pepper and salt

Cut the melon in half, scoop out the seeds and make into balls with a melon baller.

Halve and skin the avocado and cut into bite-sized slices. Pour over the juice of half a lemon and stir to coat the slices to prevent them going brown.

Quarter the soft apricots. Mix the fruits together.

Make up the dressing with the rest of the lemon juice and the other ingredients and pour over the melon mixture. Serve in glass bowls if possible. If not, you may want to dress the salad up with lettuce leaves and serve on individual plates.

Courgette timbales with cucumber and tomato salsa (Serves 7)

500g (1lb 2oz) coarsely grated courgettes
Salt
30ml (1fl oz) sunflower oil
2 eggs and one egg yolk
200ml (7fl oz) soured cream
1 tablespoon finely grated Gruyère cheese
1 tablespoon snipped fresh chives
Freshly ground black pepper

For the salsa

175g (6oz) fresh peeled, finely diced tomato
175g (6oz) finely diced cucumber
1 small, finely diced onion
1 small finely diced green chilli
25g (1oz) finely diced mild pickled gherkin
½ teaspoon sugar
1 tablespoon sherry vinegar
1 tablespoon extra virgin olive oil
Freshly ground black pepper

Put the grated courgette into a colander, sprinkle with salt and leave to drain for at least half an hour.

While the courgettes are draining, paint four 150ml (¼ pint) ramekin dishes with sunflower oil and line the bottoms with a circle of baking parchment. Oil the parchment discs.

Mix the eggs, soured cream, cheese, chives and pepper together and beat very lightly so as not to put too much air into the mix.

Squeeze out as much liquid as possible from the courgettes with your hands. Heat the sunflower oil in a wide-based pan until quite hot and stir-fry the courgettes for 5–10 minutes to cook and dry them out further. Leave to cool.

Make the salsa by mixing all the ingredients together.

Stir the cooled courgettes into the egg mixture and divide between the ramekins. Put the filled dishes into a roasting tin and pour enough hot water round them to come half way up the sides. Bake in a 150°C (130°C for a fan oven) or Gas Mark 2 oven for about 30 minutes until set.

To serve, run a thin knife round the edges of the ramekins and invert onto individual warmed plates. They will turn out readily. Remove the baking parchment and spoon some salsa beside each one. Serve warm with crusty bread.

Cucumber and smoked duck salad

250g (9oz) smoked duck breast
175g (6oz) bite-size cubed cucumber
1 large orange
A bunch of watercress

For the dressing

The juice from the orange (2–3 tablespoons)
6 tablespoons extra virgin olive oil
1 small, crushed garlic clove
The leaves picked off a large sprig of thyme
Freshly ground black pepper

If you are using a whole duck breast, slice it crossways and halve the slices if they are long, to make bite-sized pieces.

Cut the pith and skin off the oranges and divide into segments, leaving the membrane behind. Catch any juice out of the orange in a bowl and squeeze the membrane to obtain enough for the dressing.

Remove the tough thick stalks from the watercress.

Make up the dressing by putting all the ingredients into a jar and giving it a good shake to combine and thicken.

Assemble the dish by mixing the duck breast, cucumber, orange segments and most of the watercress together and dividing between four plates. Pour the dressing over and garnish with some choice sprigs of watercress.

Cocktail Bites

Spiced pumpkin seeds

100g (3½oz) raw or dried pumpkin seeds
1 small egg white
1 teaspoon Magic Masala
Pinch cayenne pepper
Pinch salt

Whisk the egg white with the spices and seasoning in a medium-sized bowl to break down the albumen. Stir in the pumpkin seeds. Drain off any excess egg white through a strainer and spread the mixture in a single layer on a non-stick baking tray. Bake in a 190°C (170°C for a fan oven) or Gas Mark 5 oven for 3 minutes. Make sure the seeds are not sticking to the tray, scrape them off if they are, and break them up. Put them back in the oven for a further 3–6 minutes, stirring a couple of times until they are browned and starting to pop. Cool and store in an airtight jar – always supposing you can resist eating them all straight away!

If you are using raw pumpkin seeds, bake the mixture in a 170°C (150°C for a fan oven) or Gas Mark 3 oven for 40 minutes or so and turn up the heat to brown for the last few minutes.

Magic Masala is a product from the New York Delhi (www.magicmasala.co.uk). You could make a homemade version by blending together a mixture of powdered mace, ground ginger, fenugreek, ground cloves, cinnamon, coriander, cumin, turmeric, cardamom and a pinch of chilli, or use a good brand medium curry powder.

Courgette cups

These little cases are extremely useful and quick to make. I have given one example of a filling but you can use anything from paté to peppers. Let your imagination run riot!

For twelve cups

2 or three largish courgettes
12 drops of Angostura bitters
120g (4oz) peeled cooked prawns (defrosted weight, if frozen)
3 tablespoons crème fraîche
1 tablespoon lemon juice
Freshly ground black pepper

Wash and cut the courgettes across into 2.5cm (1 inch) lengths. Scoop out some of the flesh, making a hollow with a good wall all round. A melon baller is the ideal tool for this job. Steam, bottom up, for 3 minutes. Put them on kitchen paper and while the cups are still warm, brush each one inside with a drop of Angostura bitters.

Chop the prawns roughly and mix with the crème fraîche, lemon juice and pepper to taste. Spoon into the cups and garnish with a flake of parsley or reserve a piece of prawn to put on top.

Melon and Parma ham balls

Once you have got the hang of these, they are very quick to make. Just remember to make the strips of Parma ham long enough to wrap round the melon balls generously. There is no need to cover the sides.

1 Galia melon
Thin slices of Parma ham
Cocktail sticks

Halve, seed and ball the melon with a melon baller. Cut strips of the Parma ham as above. Allow two melon balls per slice of ham. Wrap each melon ball with a strip of ham. With the overlapping ends upwards, secure with a cocktail stick.

Main Dishes

Pumpkin soufflé

300–400g (10–14oz) raw pumpkin
Olive oil
½ teaspoon soft brown sugar
½ teaspoon salt
20g (¾oz) butter
20g (¾oz) plain flour
200ml (7fl oz) milk
2 egg yolks
½ teaspoon chilli flakes
½ teaspoon ground ginger
1 tablespoon chopped fresh basil
50g (2oz) grated mature Manchego cheese
3 egg whites
150ml (¼ pint) double cream
1 tablespoon lime juice
2 tablespoons chopped flat-leaf parsley

Cut the pumpkin into wedges, remove the seeds and drizzle the pieces with oil. Sprinkle on the sugar and salt. Heat the oven to 180°C (160°C for a fan oven) or Gas Mark 4 and bake the pumpkin for about 45 minutes until tender. Cut the flesh from the skin and purée until smooth.

Melt the butter in a saucepan over a medium heat. Add the flour and cook for 1 minute. Gradually add the milk, stirring all the time until the sauce thickens. Cook for 3 minutes. Allow to cool a little before adding the pumpkin, egg yolks, chilli, ground ginger, basil and cheese. Mix well.

Beat the egg whites until stiff but not dry. Fold a tablespoon into the mixture in the pan to loosen it, then carefully fold in the rest of the whites. Pour the mixture into a greased soufflé dish leaving room at the top for the soufflé to rise. Put the dish into a roasting tin and fill the tin with hot water to come half way up the sides of the soufflé. Bake in a preheated oven at 180°C (160°C for a fan oven) or Gas Mark 4 for 20–30 minutes until risen and brown and set in the middle.

While it is cooking, mix the lime juice and parsley into the cream and stir until it thickens. Have your guests or family seated at the table before you take the soufflé from the oven. Serve immediately onto hot plates and serve the cream on the side.

Courgette rissoles

Makes 8 medium rissoles. I always make a big batch of these. They are a great stand-by in the freezer. You can fry them gently from frozen. They are quite fragile, so make sure a good brown crust has formed on the bottom before you turn them over in the pan. Grilled smoked bacon rashers are very good with them.

450g (1lb) shredded courgettes
Salt
1large shredded onion
1 tablespoon olive oil
Pepper
1 teaspoon Dijon mustard
150g (5oz) brown breadcrumbs
1 beaten egg
40g (1½oz) Parmesan cheese
2 tablespoons chopped mixed parsley and mint
1 tablespoon sunflower oil

Salt the shredded courgettes and drain in a colander for 30 minutes. Rinse and squeeze out as much of the juice as you can. Gently fry the courgettes and onions in the oil until the liquid has gone. Stir in the rest of the ingredients and shape into rissoles. Chill well. Fry carefully in oil until golden. Serve hot.

Courgette stuffed guinea fowl

2 oven ready guinea fowl
8 rashers smoked streaky bacon
1 tablespoon lard or sunflower oil

For the stuffing

2 medium courgettes
120g (4oz) fresh breadcrumbs
Grated zest of 1 lemon
1 chopped medium onion
120g (4oz) crumbled ricotta cheese
1 beaten egg
Pinch salt and freshly ground pepper to taste

To make the stuffing, wash and trim the courgettes and steam them
for 4 minutes. When they are cool enough to handle, cut them into
small dice.

Mix all the stuffing ingredients together to form a soft light stuffing.
Stuff the birds with this mixture. If there is any left over, put into a small
ovenproof container and place a slice of butter on top. Put into the oven
to cook for the last 20 minutes.

Cover the breast and legs of the guinea fowl with the bacon and
place in a roasting tin with the oil or fat. Roast the birds at 200°C
(180°C for a fan oven) or Gas Mark 6 for 15 minutes. Baste the fowl
and turn the oven down to 180°C (160°C for a fan oven) or Gas Mark 4.
Continue to roast the birds for another 45 minutes, basting them every
15 minutes. Check that the juices are running clear before resting them
for 15 minutes. Carve them and serve with a spoonful of stuffing, good
gravy, potatoes and a green vegetable.

Spicy squash couscous

250g (9oz) couscous
4 tablespoons olive oil
1 medium, finely chopped onion
2 fat cloves finely chopped garlic
1–2 deseeded, finely chopped red chillies
2 finely chopped carrots
2 stalks finely chopped celery
2.5cm (1 inch) grated fresh ginger
280ml (½ pint) vegetable or chicken stock
1 tablespoon sweet paprika powder
600g (1¼lb) deseeded, peeled and cubed squash
175g (6oz) peeled, cubed sweet potato
Salt and freshly ground black pepper
1 tablespoon potato flour (or cornflour) mixed with 2 tablespoons
stock or water

Make up the couscous according to the packet instructions and put into a steamer that fits exactly over the pan that you cook the stew in. Make sure you have either butter or oil stirred in. If you don't have such a steamer you can make up the couscous separately and keep it warm.

Heat the oil in a large pan. Add the finely chopped onions, garlic, chillies, carrots, celery and the grated ginger and stir-fry gently for 3 minutes. Add 3 tablespoons of the stock, cover and sweat the vegetables for 5 minutes then sprinkle in the paprika and cook for a minute or so before adding the cubed squash and sweet potato. Season with salt and freshly ground black pepper to taste. Pour in the rest of the stock, put the couscous on top of the pan and simmer for about 20 minutes until the vegetables are just tender. Remove the steamer and keep the couscous warm.

Stir the potato flour (or cornflour) into the stew. It will thicken immediately. Cook for a minute or two before checking the seasoning and spooning onto the bed of couscous in a serving dish.

Poached red bream with cucumber sauce

4 fillets red bream (or white fish fillets)
Enough fish stock to cover (or a light court-bouillon)
Cucumber and cream sauce (recipe page 86)

The fish can be any white fish fillets but I particularly like red bream if you can get it.

Skin the fillets or ask the fishmonger to do it for you. Heat the fish stock to simmering point in a wide, shallow pan and lower the fillets gently into the liquid. Keep the fish simmering for around 5–10 minutes depending on the thickness of the fillets. As soon as the fish looks opaque inside, take the pan from the heat and carefully lift the fillets with a fish slice on to hot plates. Spoon the cucumber sauce over each fillet and serve. You can use the horseradish or not, as you wish. Serve this on a bed of crushed courgettes (recipe page 60).

To make a court-bouillon, simmer a couple of slices of lemon, some salt and a few peppercorns in water for 30 minutes or so. You can use this straight away or allow to cool and refrigerate for 24 hours to help the flavour develop. If you are using a fish with a blander flavour, add some herbs, chopped onion and white wine to the pot.

Winter squash and chicken curry

500g (1lb 2oz) deseeded, peeled raw orange-fleshed squash
4 tablespoons sunflower oil
600g (1¼lb) skinned, cubed chicken breast
1 medium chopped onion
2 crushed cloves garlic
2 deseeded, sliced small hot red chillies
2.5cm (1 inch) cube of peeled and grated fresh ginger
2 heaped tablespoons good quality Thai green curry paste
Juice of 1 or 2 limes
400ml (14fl oz) coconut cream
225g (8oz) thickly sliced courgettes
Handful roughly chopped basil leaves
Salt to taste
Handful chopped coriander leaves

Chop the squash into fairly large, bite-sized cubes. Put into a roasting tin with 2 tablespoons of the sunflower oil and roast for 30 minutes until soft and slightly browned.

Heat the oil in a wide based pan. Stir-fry the chicken cubes on a high heat for 3–5 minutes until starting to brown. Remove from the pan, add the onion and fry for a minute or two then add the garlic, chillies and ginger. Stir-fry for another 3–4 minutes to cook the mixture but do not let it brown. Add the Thai curry paste to the pan and cook for a further few minutes. Add the squash cubes, the juice of one lime and the coconut cream. Put the chicken back in the pan and cook very gently for about 20 minutes by which time it should be nearly tender. Add the roasted squash to the pan with the courgettes, Stir in the basil and season to taste with salt. Cook gently for a further 5–10 minutes until the courgettes are done.

If you like the lime to be stronger, add some more juice to taste.
Serve garnished with coriander leaves.

Sarah's courgettes and their flowers with scrambled eggs

An Italian recipe from Sarah Langton-Lockton.

Sarah says that the aim is for the vegetable mixture to be perfectly cooked before adding the egg. It serves four as a light lunch and also makes a simple but elegant contribution with bruschetta, charcuterie etc. to a summer buffet. This recipe is a boon to gardeners with a glut of courgettes!

5 tablespoons olive oil
1 medium-sized chopped onion
200g (7oz) skinned, deseeded and roughly chopped firm tomatoes
450g (1lb) finely sliced courgettes
8 courgette flowers
6 beaten eggs
Salt and freshly ground pepper to taste

Heat the oil in a large, heavy-bottomed frying pan and add the onion. Fry gently until soft then add the tomatoes and courgettes. Cook for a further 20–30 minutes over a low heat. Tear the courgette flowers into several pieces and add to the pan. Cook for another 5–10 minutes until all the vegetables are tender.

Add a pinch of salt to the eggs and add to the vegetables. Cook, stirring all the time until the eggs are done. Remove from the heat, season and serve.

Stuffed marrow rings

4 large or 8 small 5cm (2 inch) deep rings of young marrow

Sausage meat stuffing

1 tablespoon vegetable oil
1 medium-sized chopped onion
1 large chopped clove garlic
450g (1lb) good quality plain pork sausage meat
1 teaspoon chopped dried mixed herbs
40g (1½oz) fresh brown breadcrumbs
1 small beaten egg
Freshly ground black pepper

Heat the vegetable oil in a large frying pan and fry the onion and garlic until soft, letting it brown a little. Add the sausage meat in small lumps together with the mixed herbs and fry, breaking up the lumps further, for 3 minutes to create a knobbly mixture. Take off the heat and stir in the breadcrumbs and beaten egg. Season with freshly ground black pepper

Vegetarian stuffing

120g (4oz) pearled spelt
1 tablespoon olive oil
1 medium-sized chopped onion
1 large chopped clove garlic
½ diced red pepper
1 tablespoon tomato ketchup
Worcester sauce
Salt and freshly ground black pepper

Rinse the spelt and put in a pan with enough water to cover it.
Simmer without salt for 15 minutes until soft. Drain and rinse,
put it in a bowl and stir in a teaspoon of olive oil to stop the grains
sticking together.

Fry the onions and garlic in olive oil as for the meat stuffing. Add the
red pepper and fry gently for a further 5 minutes.

Stir the fried vegetables into the spelt together with the tomato ketchup
and a shake or two of Worcester sauce. Season to taste with salt and
freshly ground black pepper.

Assembly

With a tablespoon, cut round the seeds in each marrow ring and
remove these to create a hollow. The curve of the spoon helps to get a
rounded hole.

Oil a baking tray lightly and place the marrow rings on the tray. Fill the
cavities with your chosen stuffing, piling it up to a mound on top. If you
are using the vegetable stuffing, cover the tray with tinfoil. Leave the meat
filling uncovered.

Bake in the oven at 180°C (160°C for a fan oven) or Gas Mark 4 for
20 minutes. The marrow flesh should have softened and the skin stayed
crunchy. Lift off the tray carefully with a fish slice and serve.

You can make a complete meal of this by preparing two rings each,
one of meat and the other of vegetable. They look very pretty sitting
side-by-side on the plate and the flavour of the fillings go very
well together.

Marrow and pork with pumpkin mash topping

50g (2oz) diced pancetta
450g (1lb) large, bite-sized chunks of pork tenderloin
1 tablespoon olive oil
1 medium-sized chopped onion
175g (6oz) button mushrooms
225g (8oz) peeled, seeded, 2.5cm (1 inch) chunks of marrow
100ml (3½fl oz) chicken stock
100ml (3½fl oz) soured cream
2 teaspoons potato flour (or cornflour)
Freshly ground black pepper

Topping

450g (1lb) buttery mashed potato
350g (12oz) pumpkin purée (recipe on page 88)
Salt and freshly ground black pepper

You will need a large pie dish for this.

Heat a wide-based, deep frying pan and fry the pancetta for a few minutes until the fat runs and it begins to brown. Remove from the frying pan and put into the pie dish.

Brown the pork on all sides and add it to the pancetta. Pour the olive oil into the pan and fry the onions for 5 minutes, add the mushrooms and fry for a further 5 minutes, then add the marrow. (If the marrow is very young and tender, there is no need to peel it). Stir-fry for a few minutes until it begins to soften. Remove from the heat and put on top of the meats.

Add the stock and soured cream into the pan and heat gently. Do not let it boil at this stage. Mix the potato flour (or cornflour) with a tablespoon of stock or water and mix into the liquids. Stir continuously until it forms a thick sauce. Season with pepper. Cook for a minute and then pour over the mixture in the pie dish.

Combine the mashed potato with the pumpkin purée and mix well. Spoon over the top of the pie dish, scratch the surface with a fork, dot with a little more butter and bake in an oven heated to 170°C (150°C for a fan oven) or Gas Mark 3 for about 30 minutes until brown and bubbling.

A meal in itself, but you could always have another green vegetable with it.

Squash and bacon pie

When it comes to pastry-making I always make my own shortcrust using a food processor, but if I want puff pastry I think the bought version saves so much time and tastes so good on the whole that I resort to that. We are lucky enough here in Dorset to have a small producer of raw pastry and you may have similar wherever you live. It is worth investigating. Buy good quality farm bacon steaks and you won't get any of the milky liquid to get in the way of your recipe.

4 x 150g (5oz) lean, dry-cured bacon steaks
225g (8oz) peeled, seeded, bite-sized cubes of squash
450g (1lb) puff pastry
1 tablespoon rapeseed or vegetable oil
1 medium chopped onion
1 crushed clove garlic
1 small glass dry white wine
1 x 400g (14oz) can chopped tomatoes
½ teaspoon mixed dried herbs
Freshly ground black pepper
225g (8oz) trimmed, thickly sliced courgettes
A little beaten egg

Remove most but not all the bacon fat from the steaks and cut into 2.5cm (1 inch) cubes.

Steam the cubes of squash for 7–8 minutes to start softening them.

Roll out the pastry and lay a 1.2 litre (2 pint) pie dish, top down, onto it and cut round the dish, leaving about 1cm (½ inch) overlap. Lift the dish off. Keep the remaining scraps for making up the pie. Put the pastry in the fridge while you make the filling.

Heat the oil in a wide-based lidded pan and when it is smoking hot, add the bacon. Stir-fry for 3–5 minutes until it starts to brown and give off a little fat. Reduce the heat to medium, add the onion and garlic and fry with the bacon for 5 minutes until the vegetables are soft. Add the white wine, tomatoes, herbs and black pepper and simmer gently until the sauce has thickened – about 15 minutes. Mix in the partly cooked squash and the courgettes and tip the mixture into a pie dish. The dish should be full. Allow to cool for 30 minutes.

Top the pie with the pastry in the usual way. Paint with the beaten egg and bake at 200°C (180°C for a fan oven) or Gas Mark 6 for the first 10 minutes, then turn down to 180°C (160°C for a fan oven) or Gas Mark 4 and bake for 30 minutes until the pastry is puffed and golden.

I have recently become a fan of rapeseed oil. It is healthy, very versatile and adds a wonderful nutty flavour to dishes. The English answer to olive oil. Try it.

Marinated beef and courgette skewers on coriander rice

450g (1lb) fillet, sirloin or rump steak
About 24 thick slices, unpeeled courgette

Marinade

2.5cm (1 inch) knob of finely grated fresh ginger
2 stalks finely chopped lemon grass
2 tablespoons dark soy sauce
2 large crushed cloves garlic
1 teaspoon freshly ground black pepper
1 teaspoon sugar
2 tablespoons rapeseed or sunflower oil

For the rice

1 tablespoon rapeseed or sunflower oil
2 large, finely chopped shallots
1 large finely chopped clove garlic
225g (8oz) white basmati rice
4 thinly sliced spring onions
1 litre (2 pints) of hot water
Salt and freshly ground black pepper
Lots of chopped coriander

Trim some of the fat from the beef, if necessary. Cut the meat into large cubes about 4cm (1½ inch) square. Mix all the ingredients for the marinade in a large bowl and marinate the beef in it for 3–5 hours.

I use long metal skewers for this but if you want to use wooden skewers, soak them in cold water for 30 minutes – you may need two per person if they are quite short.

In a lidded frying pan, heat the rapeseed oil and stir-fry the shallots and garlic over a medium heat until golden brown. Add the rice and stir around until it is coated with the oil, shallots and garlic mixture then add about 550ml (1 pint) of hot water. Stir, then leave to simmer until the rice has absorbed the water. From now on add hot water when necessary, risotto style, until the rice is done. Stir in the spring onion, seasoning and coriander, put the lid on the pan and keep warm while the skewers cook.

Heat the grill to medium hot. Thread the courgette slices and beef alternately onto the skewers, starting and ending with a slice of courgette and packing the skewers tightly. Brush the skewers with the marinade and grill for about 3 minutes on each side until nicely browned and cooked to your liking. Serve on a bed of the rice.

Crown roast of lamb with squash stuffing

This is a wonderful dish for a celebratory occasion. It is certainly not cheap, especially if you want to use the new season's English lamb, but I think it is well worth it.

A 12-chop crown roast of lamb with any trimmings

For the stuffing

225g (8oz) peeled, seeded butternut squash
1 tablespoon sunflower oil
1 medium, halved sliced onion
120g (4oz) fresh breadcrumbs
Grated rind of 1 lemon
2 tablespoons chopped parsley
50g (2oz) chopped walnuts
2 tablespoons squash or pumpkin purée
Salt and freshly ground black pepper to taste
1 well-beaten egg

Ask your butcher to give you the trimmings from preparing the crown roast. He may have stuffed some of them into the middle of the joint and that will be useful for you.

Cut the squash into small cubes, about 1cm (½ inch). Heat the oil in a wide pan. Fry the onion until it begins to soften then add the squash cubes. Turn the heat up and stir-fry the mixture until the onion and squash are browned.

Put the breadcrumbs into a bowl. Add the lemon rind, parsley, nuts and squash mixture and season to taste.

Drain and discard any excess water that may have collected round the squash purée and stir the purée into the egg. Add this to the bowl to bind all the ingredients together.

Remove the trimmings from the crown roast. Bind the tips of the bones with foil to stop them burning and place the joint in an oiled roasting tin. Press as much of the stuffing into the middle cavity as possible, packing it tightly. Take a piece of the trimmings and put on the top, covering the stuffing generously. You will have a lot of stuffing left so grease an ovenproof dish and add the left-over mixture. Press it down and cover it with more of the trimmings. This protects the stuffing and adds flavour to it.

Roast the crown in a preheated oven at 200°C (180°C for a fan oven) or Gas Mark 6 for 10 minutes then turn the oven down to 180°C (160°C for a fan oven) or Gas Mark 4 for a further 20 minutes. Rest for 15 minutes before carving.

Serve with a redcurrant jelly flavoured gravy, potatoes and some vegetables.

Side Dishes

Crushed courgettes with basil

450g (1lb) courgettes
A little butter
Roughly chopped leaves from two or three basil stems

Cut the courgettes into approximately 2.5cm (1 inch) rounds and steam for 5 minutes or so, until they are tender in the middle but the outsides are still crisp. Put them into a colander and crush them roughly with a potato masher. (The idea is to get a mixture of textures.)

Tip them into a pan containing a little melted butter, and stir over a low heat to coat them with the fat. Stir in the roughly chopped basil and serve.

Roasted marrow

Roasting really brings the best out of a marrow.

1kg (2lb 2oz) peeled, deseeded marrow flesh
Salt
Olive oil
Freshly ground black pepper

Cut the marrow into 3cm (1¼ inch) cubes, put them into a colander, sprinkle with salt, mix and leave to drain for at least 30 minutes. Rinse and dry them on kitchen paper.

When you have removed as much moisture as possible, tip the cubes out into a non-stick roasting tin that will hold them in one layer. Put them into an oven heated to 110°C (90°C for a fan oven) or Gas Mark ¼ for up to an hour to dry them even further.

Turn the oven heat up to 220°C (200°C for a fan oven) or Gas Mark 7. Drizzle some olive oil over the cubes and toss them to coat. Roast for 15 minutes until they start getting brown at the edges. Sprinkle with freshly ground black pepper and they are ready to serve.

Good with salty meat such as bacon steak or tongue as well as fish and other more delicate-tasting foods.

Marrow in mustard sauce

700g (1½lb) peeled, deseeded marrow
4 tablespoons rapeseed or sunflower oil
150g (5oz) crème fraîche
Tablespoon of Dijon mustard
Juice of ½ lemon
Salt and freshly ground black pepper

Cut the marrow into large, bite-sized cubes. Heat the oil in a frying pan and fry the marrow over a medium heat for 4–5 minutes until it starts to soften. Mix the crème fraîche, mustard and lemon juice together and pour over the marrow. Stir and add the seasoning to taste. Heat gently and serve.

This is a very useful recipe in that you can add different herbs, depending on what you are serving it with. Add dill or tarragon for fish, basil or parsley with tomato-based dishes, etc. However, it is also delicious as it is.

Pumpkin chips

700g (1½lb) peeled, deseeded, quartered pumpkin
1 tablespoon rapeseed oil
1 teaspoon coarsely ground black pepper
½ teaspoon ras-el hanout powder
1 small pinch chilli powder

Cut the pumpkin into chips roughly the same size. Put in a roasting
tin with the rapeseed oil, sprinkle with the spices and roll them around
with your hands to coat them. Roast them in an oven heated to 220°C
(200°C for a fan oven) or Gas Mark 7 for about 15 minutes until they are
nice and brown. They will not get crisp but, if my family get near these,
I usually double-up the recipe! They are to die for!

Ras-el hanout is a complex Moroccan spice mixture that is now more
readily available in supermarkets and delicatessens. If you have trouble
finding it, go to www.seasonedpioneers.co.uk. They have wonderful
spice products.

Sautéed courgettes

600g (1¼lbs) trimmed courgettes, diagonally cut in 2cm (¾ inch) slices
1 tablespoon plain flour
4 tablespoons finely grated Parmesan or Manchego cheese
1 pinch of smoked hot paprika
4 tablespoons olive or rapeseed oil

Steam the courgettes for 3 minutes. Tip them onto kitchen paper and spread them out flat to drain. Cover with another layer of kitchen paper to dry the tops.

Mix the flour, cheese and paprika together on a large plate. Press the cut sides of the courgettes into the mixture to coat them.

Heat the oil over a medium-hot heat and fry the courgette slices on each side until golden brown.

Very good with any grilled or roasted meat.

Pan-fried cucumber with garlic and ginger

1 large peeled, halved lengthways and seeded cucumber
1cm (½ inch) knob of peeled fresh ginger
2 cloves garlic
10g (½oz) butter
1 tablespoon olive or rapeseed oil
1 finely chopped shallot
1 pinch of chilli powder
Salt and freshly ground black pepper

Cut the cucumber halves into 1cm (½ inch) half-moons. Very finely slice the ginger. (Try using a mandolin for this if you have one.) Finely slice the garlic.

Heat the butter and oil in large frying pan and gently fry the shallot until it is transparent. Turn up the heat to high and add the cucumber. Stir-fry for 2–3 minutes before adding the garlic and ginger. Fry for another minute. Remove from the heat and add the seasonings to taste.

Try this with chicken or fish.

Jen's maple glazed squash

Americans have a great affinity with squashes. This is another great recipe from Jennifer Bushman.

60ml (2fl oz) olive oil
450g (1lb) peeled, cubed butternut squash
60ml (2fl oz) maple syrup
2 tablespoons chopped flat-leaf parsley
2 tablespoons finely grated Parmesan cheese
Salt and freshly ground black pepper

Heat the oil in a wide-based pan over a medium heat. Add the squash, cover and cook, stirring occasionally, for about 10 minutes until just tender and a little brown. Add the maple syrup and toss until the squash is shiny with glaze. Add the parsley, cheese, and salt and pepper to taste.

Grilled chayote with other squashes

Chayotes, known as Christophenes in the States, have a limited season in this country. They are smooth, pale green-skinned with a soft single seed in the middle. You can usually get them in a supermarket in the summer but if you have access to a Caribbean food shop you will find them at other times. They are a fairly bland but interesting addition to the squash family, so do try them.

60ml (2fl oz) lime juice
1 teaspoon hot smoked paprika powder
1 teaspoon ground cumin
60ml (2fl oz) olive oil
1 peeled, seeded and wedged chayote squash
½ small peeled, thickly sliced butternut or other squash
2 large, thickly sliced lengthways, courgettes
2 quartered ripe tomatoes
1 large peeled and wedged red onion
 Salt and freshly ground black pepper

If you can find yellow courgettes, use one to add to this colourful dish.

For the marinade

Whisk the first three ingredients in small bowl. Add the oil and whisk until well blended.

Prepare a barbecue to medium-high heat, or heat the indoor grill to a medium-hot heat. Place all vegetables on a baking tray. Brush with the marinade mixture and leave until you are ready to cook it. Grill until tender and beginning to brown, turning occasionally and basting with more marinade. Grill for 5–10 minutes for tomatoes, courgettes and onion and 15 minutes for chayote and other squash.

Quite a tongue-tingling addition to grilled meats and fish.

Spicy creamed cucumber

Whereas the vast majority of my recipes are reasonably healthy, this is a wonderfully decadent concoction! Lovely with hot and cold meats as well as white fish. With a little added milk and the cucumber diced, you can use it as a sauce.

1½ large peeled, quartered lengthways, seeded cucumbers
50g (2oz) butter
1 teaspoon medium-hot curry powder
200ml (7fl oz) double cream
3 egg yolks
1 tablespoon balsamic vinegar
1 dessertspoonful lemon juice
Salt and freshly ground black pepper
1 pinch of cayenne pepper

Cut the quarters of cucumber in half again lengthways then cut them across into roughly 5cm (2 inch) sticks. Steam them for two minutes.

Heat the butter in a frying pan and add the curry powder. Cook, stirring for a minute before adding the cucumber sticks. Fry, stirring frequently for 5 minutes then pour in the cream. Let it bubble and reduce a little.

Mix the egg yolks with the vinegar and lemon juice. Take a tablespoon of hot sauce and stir it into the egg and stir this into the pan. Heat very gently, stirring all the time, until the sauce thickens slightly. Do not let it boil. Season to taste with the salt, pepper and cayenne.

Salads

Melon, cucumber and lemon chicken salad

Grated rind and juice of 1 large lemon
½ teaspoon sugar
6 tablespoons plain yoghurt
3 tablespoons rapeseed oil
2 large or 4 small chicken breasts
Melon balls from one medium-sized Galia melon
175g (6oz) diced, unpeeled cucumber
225g (8oz) cubed, unpeeled cooked new potatoes
1 small deseeded diced red pepper
1 tablespoon chopped mint leaves

Mix the juice and rind of the lemon, the sugar, yoghurt and rapeseed oil together to make a marinade – it also doubles as a dressing. Marinate the chicken breasts for at least 2 hours in half the marinade in a non-metallic ovenproof dish that will hold them in one layer.

Heat a griddle pan until very hot. Remove the chicken breasts from the marinade and place them on the griddle. Leave alone to brown for 2–3 minutes before turning them over and doing the same on the other side. Put them back in the marinade in the ovenproof dish. Preheat the oven to 180°C (160°C for a fan oven) or Gas Mark 4 and bake the breasts for about 15–30 minutes until cooked through. Drain them on kitchen paper and cool.

In a serving bowl, mix together the melon, cucumber, potato and red pepper. Cut the chicken into large dice and mix into the other ingredients. Pour over the reserved marinade as a dressing and toss well. Serve sprinkled with the mint leaves.

Roasted squash salad

2 tablespoons sunflower oil
700g (1½lbs) peeled, deseeded and cubed onion or butternut squash
1 tablespoon lime juice
1 small crushed clove garlic
3 tablespoons extra virgin olive oil
A pinch of sugar
6 thinly sliced spring onions
A handful of chopped flat-leaf parsley

Put the sunflower oil, and squash cubes in a roasting tin and roast at 220°C (200°C for a fan oven) or Gas Mark 7 until soft and browned. Allow to cool a little. Mix together the lime juice, garlic, olive oil and sugar. Use to dress the cooled squash cubes. Sprinkle over the chopped spring onion and the parsley when the salad is cold and serve.

Courgette salad

Another very simple but delicious dish that helps to keep your courgette plants from inundating you with a glut.

600g (1¼lbs) baby courgettes, no longer than 10cm (4 inches) long and the thickness of a cigar
Juice of ½ large lemon
1 crushed clove garlic
6 tablespoons extra virgin olive oil
Salt and freshly ground black pepper
Good pinch smoked mild paprika
Chopped parsley

Trim the ends of the courgettes and steam for 4–5 minutes, leaving them with a little crunch. Make up the dressing with everything but the parsley. Cut the courgettes into quarters lengthways while still hot and dress them. Add the chopped parsley before serving.

Sinnet's Danish cucumber salad

Sinnet says, "This is delicious with meat stews and paprika-based dishes like Goulash and Beouf Stroganoff."

1 smooth-skinned cucumber
Garlic (optional)
200ml (7fl oz) single cream
Juice of ½ large lemon
A pinch of sugar
Salt and freshly ground black pepper (optional)

Slice the cucumber into paper-thin slices. Use a mandolin if you have one. Put the cucumber into a colander and allow to drain. (You can salt them at this stage to aid the draining but personally, I think it spoils the consistency.)

If you are using the garlic, rub a cut clove all over the surface of your serving dish to give just a hint of flavour. Empty the cream into the serving dish and stir in the lemon juice to thicken it but don't let it curdle. Mix in the seasonings and toss in the drained cucumber.

This salad is also extremely good with fish or as a salad in its own right.

Squash, melon and avocado salad

1 peeled, seeded and cubed butternut or other squash
1 Galia melon
2 small avocado pears
1 tablespoon lime juice (and a squeeze for the avocado)
½ very finely chopped medium-hot red chilli
1 teaspoon peeled, very finely chopped fresh ginger
3 tablespoons walnut oil
Chopped parsley for garnish

Steam the squash until tender, about 10 minutes. Halve the melon and make into balls with a melon baller. Peel and stone the avocados. Cut the flesh into bite-size slices and squeeze over some lime juice to stop it discolouring. Mix these ingredients together in a bowl.

Whisk the lime juice, chilli, ginger and oil to make a dressing, pour over the squash mixture and toss. Add the chopped parsley for garnish and serve.

Jo Andrews's pumpkin, red pepper and onion salad

Jo was given this recipe by a friend and near neighbour while she was living in New Zealand. It is slightly adapted.

1 medium 120g (4oz) red onion
1 large red pepper
400g (14oz) peeled, seeded and cubed butternut squash
2 tablespoons rapeseed or sunflower oil
Small bunch roughly chopped coriander

For the dressing

Juice of 1 lemon
2–3 cloves crushed garlic
1 tablespoon balsamic vinegar
3 tablespoons extra virgin olive oil
Salt and freshly ground black pepper

Peel the red onion and cut vertically into 8 wedges. Halve the red pepper, remove the core and seeds and cut into 1cm (½ inch) half-moons.

Put all the vegetables on a baking tray and coat with the oil. Roast in an oven heated to 180°C (160°C for a fan oven) or Gas Mark 4 for 20 minutes. Stir the mixture and cook for a further 10 minutes or so until tender. Make up the dressing and pour over the warm vegetables. Leave till cold before serving, garnished with the chopped coriander.

Cucumber and mint ring with watermelon and avocado salad

This is about the most versatile recipe I can think of. It is lovely with the salad here but you can fill the centre with anything that takes your fancy. A chicken salad, a seafood salad – the possibilities are endless. This recipe serves 6–8 as a starter or 4–6 as a main course salad. It makes a great addition to a buffet table.

1 large peeled, coarsely grated cucumber
1 teaspoon sunflower oil
6 finely sliced spring onions, both white and pale green parts
150ml (¼ pint) vegetable or chicken stock
1 packet (½ tablespoon) powdered gelatine
200g (7oz) cream cheese
100g (3½oz) crème fraîche
Juice of 1 lime
1 heaped tablespoon finely chopped mint, plus a few sprigs
for garnish
Salt and white pepper to taste

Salad

1 large ripe, peeled and chopped avocado pear
Juice of ½ lime
300g (10oz) peeled, seeded and cubed watermelon
Salt and freshly ground black pepper
About a dozen finely snipped chives
1 tablespoon rapeseed or walnut oil

You will need a 20cm (8 inch) ring mould for this.

Put the grated cucumber into a colander while you assemble and prepare the rest of the ingredients. You don't need it to be very well drained.

Gently fry the spring onions in the sunflower oil until soft. Set aside. Heat the stock in a small pan. Sprinkle the gelatine on top and stir until it has melted. Alternatively, melt the gelatine by your usual method.

Beat the cream cheese and crème fraîche until smooth. Stir in the cucumber, spring onions, lime juice, chopped mint and salt and pepper. Strain the gelatine and stock into the bowl, stirring all the time.

Rinse the ring mould in cold water but do not dry. Pour the mixture into the ring and refrigerate until set. Make sure the mould is not absolutely brim full so that the set ring will turn out easily.

Make up the salad by coating the avocado with the lime juice and mixing in the rest of the ingredients in a bowl.

When ready to serve, run a thin palette knife round the top edge of the mould to loosen it. Invert a serving plate on top and turn the whole thing over. Pick up the plate, holding the ring in the middle of it and give it a shake. It ought to drop out onto the plate. If by any chance it is stubborn, soak the outside of the ring briefly in a basin of hot water – 10 seconds will be enough – and try again.

Spoon the salad into the centre of the ring and arrange the rest round about. Garnish with sprigs of mint.

Courgettes with cos lettuce

The use of yellow courgettes in this recipe is purely cosmetic, so replace with more green ones if you can't get the yellow. Some wedges of hard-boiled egg are a nice addition to this.

350g (12oz) mixed green and yellow courgettes
Juice of ½ lime
Juice of ½ lemon
1 heaped tablespoon chopped dill
Sliced heart of 1 cos lettuce
25g (1oz) toasted pumpkin seeds

For the dressing

1 teaspoon clear honey
Juice of ½ lime
3 tablespoons rapeseed oil
Salt and freshly ground black pepper to taste

Chop the courgettes into small dice. Pour over the lemon and lime juice and leave to marinate for 30 minutes. Don't leave them much longer or the water will start to seep out of them. Stir in the chopped dill and mix in the crunchy cos lettuce. Whisk up the dressing ingredients and pour over the salad. Garnish with toasted pumpkin seeds.

Desserts
&
Sweet
Things

Pumpkin and blood orange tart

Pastry

For a 20cm (8 inch) pie dish:

120g (4oz) plain flour
80g (3oz) butter
1 tablespoon icing sugar
1 egg yolk
A little very cold water

Filling

Grated rind and thinly sliced flesh of 1 blood orange
75ml (3fl oz) blood orange juice
1 tablespoon caster sugar
120g (4oz) steamed pumpkin purée (recipe page 88)
1 whole egg and two egg yolks

Glaze

1 tablespoon caster sugar

Make up the pastry in your favourite way. (I make mine in a food processor.)

Leave to chill in the fridge for at least 30 minutes before rolling out,
lining your pie dish and baking blind until light golden brown and crisp.

Mix the rind and juice of the oranges and the caster sugar with the
pumpkin purée. Beat the egg and additional yolks well and stir into
the mixture.

Pour the filling into the pastry case and very carefully arrange the blood
orange slices on top.

Bake in a slow oven, 150°C (130°C for a fan oven) or Gas Mark 2 for about
30 minutes until set. Allow to cool a little, then sprinkle the surface with a
tablespoon of caster sugar and brown it with a blow torch or under a hot grill
until the orange slices create a dark brown pattern. Serve hot, warm or cold.

You can make this with ordinary oranges but it isn't quite so good.

Melon and ginger fruit salad

Simple and quick to make, this is a dish the can be stretched to large quantities for parties.

600g (1¼lbs) different colours of melon – water, Galia, cantaloupe, etc
½ –1 piece of very finely chopped stem ginger
1 tablespoon stem ginger syrup
2 tablespoons Muscat wine or white port
Chopped mint leaves

Cut up the melons into bite-sized pieces in various shapes. Use a melon baller to scoop out one, cut another type into small slices, another into cubes.

Add the rest of the ingredients and mix well.

The secret to this lies in not using too much ginger. It is very easy to drown the taste of the melon. Serve well chilled with a dish of crème fraîche or Greek-style yoghurt. For supper or dinner parties, this looks and tastes lovely in individual glasses with the crème fraîche or yoghurt spooned on top and decorated with pumpkin seed praline (Recipe page 90).

Squash mousse

350g (12oz) peeled, deseeded, cubed squash flesh
75g (2½oz) caster sugar
7.5cm (3 inch) piece of cinnamon stick
1 small knob fresh ginger
1 pinch freshly grated nutmeg
2 teaspoons powdered gelatine
3 tablespoons water
3 tablespoons lemon juice
1 tablespoon stem ginger syrup
3 eggs
250ml (9fl oz) double cream
Pumpkin seed praline to decorate (recipe page 90)

This quantity fills a 1 litre (2 pint) soufflé dish. Put the empty dish into the
fridge before you start.

Put the squash, sugar and spices into a pan with about 275ml (½ pint)
of water. Bring to the boil and simmer until the squash is very tender and
the liquid reduced to a syrupy consistency. This takes ½–¾ hour.

Sprinkle the gelatine onto 3 tablespoons of water in a small bowl.
Leave to soak for 5 minutes then melt over hot water.

When the squash is ready, tip it with the lemon juice and stem ginger
syrup into a blender and blitz until smooth. Pour the mixture into a large
bowl and allow to cool a little.

Separate the eggs and beat the yolks into the purée then stir in the
melted gelatine. Refrigerate for about 15–30 minutes until the mixture
begins to thicken.

Whip the cream until thick and fold into the purée. Whip the egg whites
until you get a soft peak. Fold in a couple of spoonfuls of egg white
to loosen the mixture, then fold in the rest. Pour into the cold dish and
return to the fridge to chill well. Just before serving, sprinkle with a good
coating of pumpkin seed praline.

Everyone will want second helpings!

Courgette cake

250g (9oz) coarsely grated courgettes
2 large eggs
120g (4oz) caster sugar
120ml (4fl oz) rapeseed oil
225g (8oz) self-raising flour
1 teaspoon baking powder
1 pinch each of cinnamon and freshly grated nutmeg
1 pinch of salt
All but one teaspoonful of the zest of one large orange

Filling

120g (4oz) softened unsalted butter
225g (8oz) icing sugar
1 teaspoon orange zest
The juice of half the large orange

Put the grated courgettes into a colander and leave to drain for 30 minutes. Do not salt. Using your hands, squeeze out as much of the liquid as possible.

In the electric mixer bowl, beat the eggs and caster sugar until they thicken and then beat in the rapeseed oil. The mixture ought to be the consistency of thick double cream.

Sift the flour, baking powder, spices and salt into the egg mixture and continue to beat until really well blended. Stir in the courgettes and orange zest. Pour the mixture into two 20cm (8 inch) greased and lined cake tins and bake in a 170°C (150°C for a fan oven) or Gas Mark 3 oven. Keep the oven door closed for 25 minutes and then test the cakes with your fingers. They should be firm to the touch. If not, bake for a further 5 minutes or so. Leave in the tins for a few minutes before turning out onto a wire rack to cool.

Make the icing by beating together the butter and icing sugar and stirring in the zest and orange juice to make a light butter cream. When the cakes are cold, spread the filling over one cake and sandwich the other on top. Sprinkle the top with icing sugar if you like.

This cake keeps well in an airtight tin. It is equally as good with lemon or lime flavouring.

Marrow and ginger preserve

800g (1lb 12oz) prepared marrow
450ml (¾ pint) water
600g (1¼lbs) preserving or granulated sugar
1 large knob of stem ginger
1 tablespoon stem ginger syrup
Juice of 1 large lemon
3 strips lemon rind

To prepare the marrow, peel it thoroughly so that any of the whiter flesh just under the skin is removed, too. Cut it in half lengthways, scoop out the seeds and soft middle part and cut into small cubes about 1cm (½ inch).

Boil the marrow in the water for 15 minutes until beginning to soften. Remove with a slotted spoon into a colander sitting in a deep plate. Add the rest of the ingredients to the pan, stir to melt the sugar and simmer for a few minutes to infuse the flavours.

Put the marrow back in the pan, together with any liquid collected in the plate. Bring to the boil and simmer for about 1½ hours until the marrow is transparent.

This preserve is not meant to set. Use it to pour over ice cream or other puddings such as a gateau. Stir some into a fruit salad for a different taste.

It's yummy! I have taken to adding a sachet of pectin lately, to thicken the syrup a little more.

Sundries

Cucumber and cream sauce

A lovely sauce with any white fish.

7.5cm (3 inch) piece of cucumber
Salt
10g (½oz) butter
150ml (¼ pint) double cream
1 teaspoon horseradish (optional)
Freshly ground black pepper

Grate the cucumber on a large gauge grater. Sprinkle with a little salt and leave to drain for 30 minutes then squeeze out as much moisture as possible.

Melt the butter in a small pan, add the cucumber and simmer gently for a minute or two. Stir in the cream and horseradish, if you are using it and season with black pepper.

Anna's courgette flower sauce for pasta

Anna tells me that you can buy courgette flowers in season in some specialist food stores if you don't grow your own courgettes. She also says she has used this sauce to accompany white fish.

12 washed, finely chopped courgette flowers
1 small finely chopped onion
Bunch of finely chopped flat-leaf parsley
4 tablespoons olive oil
Pinch of saffron powder or a few saffron strands
4 tablespoons hot, light vegetable stock
Salt and freshly ground black pepper
1 large free-range egg yolk
75g (2½oz) freshly grated pecorino cheese

Mix the courgette flowers, onion and parsley together. Sauté gently in half the olive oil in a pan for about 10 minutes, stirring frequently.

Dissolve the saffron in the hot stock and then add to the pan. Stir well and cook for a further 10 minutes. Add salt and pepper to taste and then purée the sauce in a food processor or blender.

Use the rest of the olive oil to toss into your chosen cooked pasta, then mix the egg yolk and pecorino cheese into the sauce and pour it over the pasta.

Steamed squash (or pumpkin) purée

I find it so useful to have some squash purée in the freezer. I use it to make a quick soup or stir it into stock to make a vegetable risotto as well as being able to serve it as a vegetable. I leave it very plain so that I can add flavours and seasonings to it.

Just peel, deseed and cut up any kind of winter squash or pumpkin and steam it until it is tender, then whiz up in a blender or food processor to a purée. Freeze in smallish quantities and use it as and when you need it. You may find it collects some water round it if it has been frozen. It is best to drain this off unless you want a rather loose consistency.

Pumpkin chutney

1.25kg (2½lbs) peeled and deseeded pumpkin
600g (1¼lbs) peeled and cored cooking apple
1 thinly sliced unpeeled orange
80g (3oz) peeled fresh ginger
3 deseeded red Thai chillies
3 tablespoons black mustard seeds
2 tablespoons sweet paprika
1.2 litres (2 pints) cider vinegar
600g (1¼lbs) light brown sugar
1 tablespoon salt

Sterilise your chosen lidded jam jars (the mixture should make about 4lb) by putting them into a hot oven or through the dishwasher.

Put all the ingredients apart from the sugar and salt into a preserving pan. Mix well, bring to the boil and simmer until the pumpkin is just tender (20–30 minutes).

Add the sugar and salt and stir until they have melted. Simmer until the mixture is thick, stirring from time to time.

Heat your jars and spoon the chutney into them. Put a wax paper on top and seal the jars. Store for at least four weeks before using.

Pumpkin seed praline

80g (3oz) caster sugar
50g (2oz) pumpkin seeds

If, like myself, you keep seeds and nuts in the freezer to keep them fresh, put the pumpkin seeds into a low oven for an hour to crisp them up a little. This is optional but I find it beneficial.

Put the sugar and seeds into a pan over a low heat. The sugar will soon begin to melt. Watch it carefully to make sure it doesn't burn. When it is nearly melted, stir it with a metal spoon until the mixture becomes a good dark-golden colour. Pour the mixture onto a piece of oiled baking parchment on a heatproof plate and leave to get cold. As soon as it is brittle, break it into pieces and store in an airtight container. It should last a month or two. Crush it as you need it.

The pieces can be eaten as a sweet. It's yummy!

Index
of
Recipes

Index of Recipes